It's great
part of

S T I C

Artwork by Peter Vegas
Published by Santoro Graphics

First published in UK by Santoro Graphics Ltd in 2006
Santoro Graphics Ltd
Rotunda Point
11 Hartfield Crescent
Wimbledon
London
SW19 3RL

Copyright ©2006 Santoro. All rights reserved.

ISBN: 1 90111 912 2

Greeting cards also available from Santoro Graphics Ltd
UK tel: (01709) 518100
www.santorographics.com
For licensing opportunities please contact licensing@santorographics.com

Welcome along to the second book of Stickmen.

The first one was internationally acclaimed. When I say internationally acclaimed, I mean I sent my uncle Rod a copy - he liked it and he lives overseas. So there you go. Anyway, welcome along to Book 2. The fabulous follow up. The super sequel.

When my publisher said we were going to do a second book, I said cool. I had heaps of new stickman ideas lying around and mum needs a hip operation. Then they said we need you to write another intro and I was stumped. What could I write about in the new book? I've already explained my early childhood fascination with stickmen in Book 1. If you haven't read that you really need to buy a copy. And I'm not just saying that to make you go out and buy a copy of the first book...... Ok, I am. But hey, like I said, mum needs a hip operation. I'll tell you what, if you go and buy 5000 copies of either Book One or Book Two, then I'll get my mum to name one of her hips after you. How's that for an offer? Right, well that's enough from me, you didn't come here to read long blathering intros, you came for a quick fix of stickman humour. So off you go. Dive in and have a laugh - have a few, we've sprinkled them liberally throughout the book. Here's to stickmen and the ever increasing cost of good hip operations.

This book is dedicated to my mum's hips.

Peter Vegas January 2006

Stickman with multiple personalities

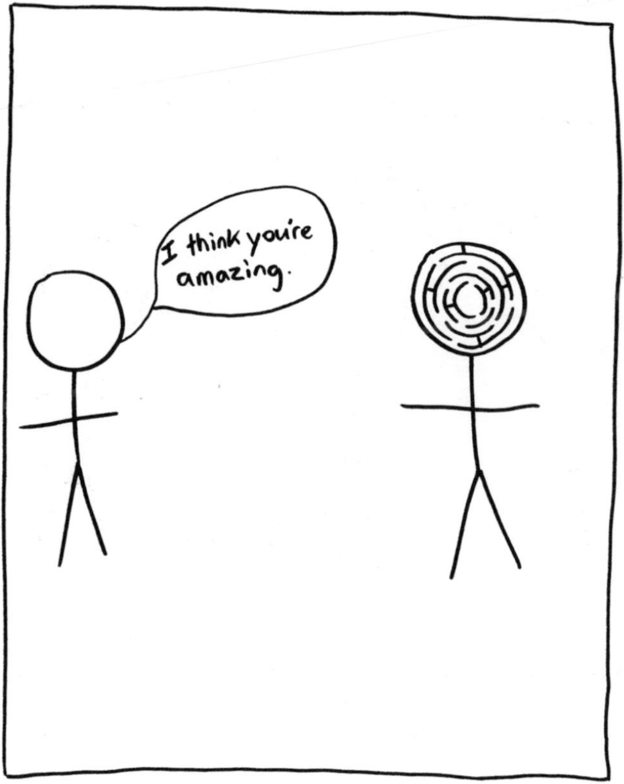
I think you're amazing.

Tip #1 - Keep your head on
your shoulders.

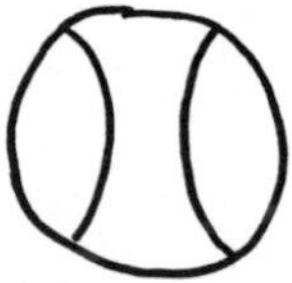

Two stickmen trying to look out of a porthole.

Stickman in Space

Princess Leia

Halfwit

Florist

Stickman holding a present.

William Tell's son

Tip # 4 You can never own enough power tools.
Honey I need a new electric drill

tribe of head hunters

Tip #5 Its good to stay flexible

Air traffic controller

Butterfly collector

Tip # 6   Life is just one big game.

equestrian

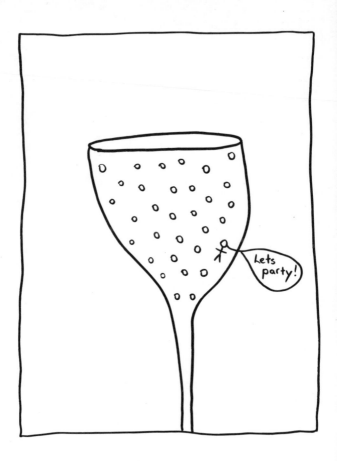

<u>contortionist in a box</u>

Tip #7 Think about others

||0||00||0|0||0|0|10||00||100||0||0|0||0

Bill Gates

Walt Disney

Stickman holding a Kite

Tip #8 A woman can never have enough pairs of shoes

The three wise men

Deep Sea Diver

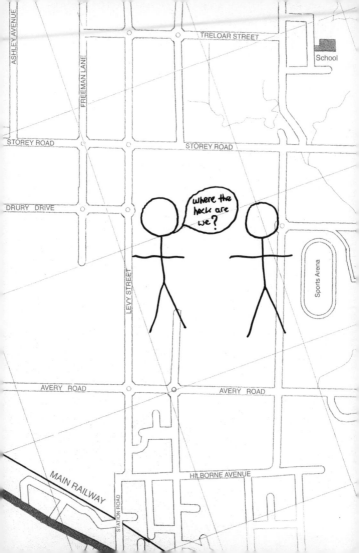

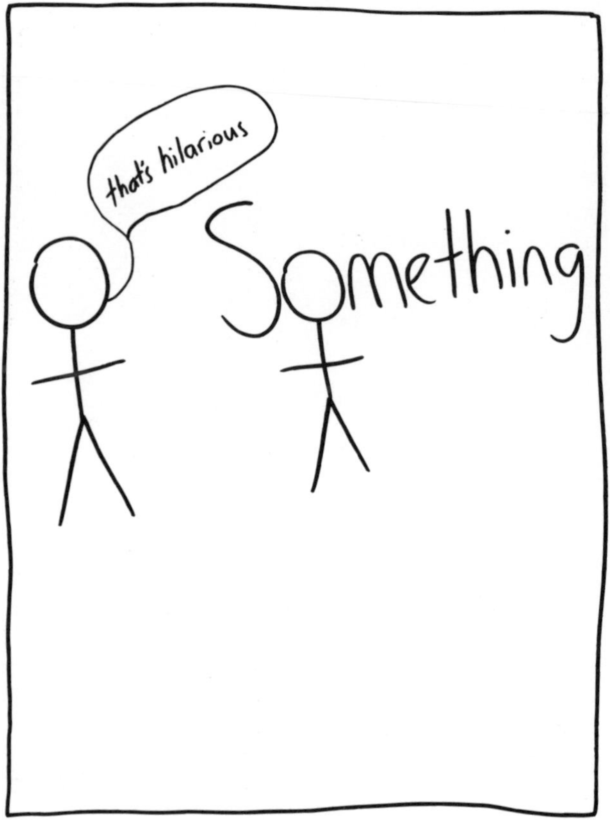

Stickman with a degree.

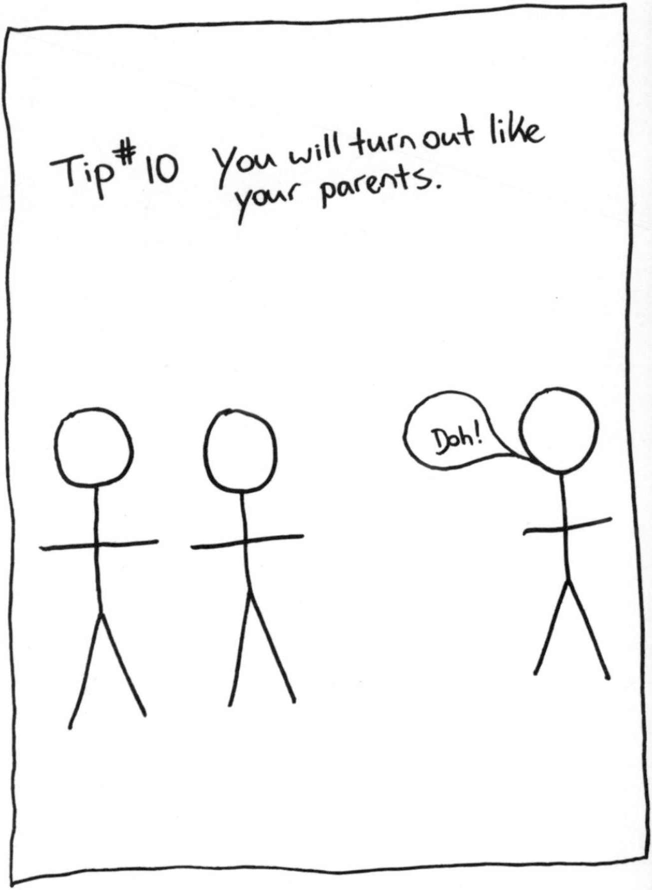
Tip# 10 You will turn out like your parents.
Doh!

<u>cheerleader or weightlifter</u>

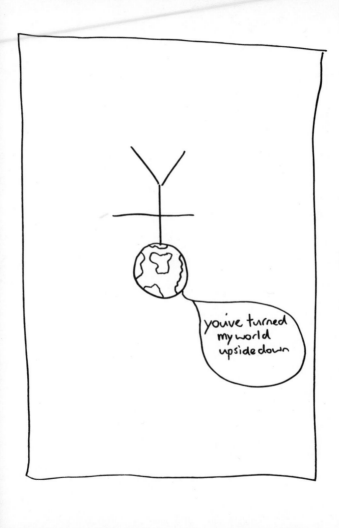

Tip #11 The world doesn't need any more DJs.

stickman with Botox

Tip #12 Get plenty of sleep.

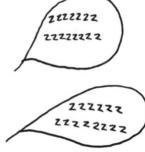

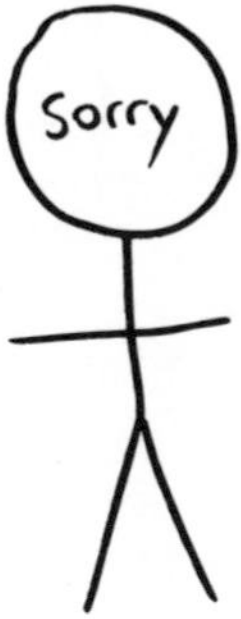

Stickman filled with sorrow

Tip #13 At sea, from a long way away people look like little balls

Stickman waiting for a hip replacement